MW00388590

All Rights Reserved

Disclaimer

Your Disclaimer or legal notices can go here...

50 Gluten & Sugar Free Recipes
So Good They Won't Know It's Healthy

By Christopher D Guebert
My Green Earth LLC
With Frederico Braho

Introduction

Hi, I'm Chris. I decided to put this book together because there are not enough gluten free, sugar free good recipes out there. I recruited a talented chef to help, Frederico Braho (Freddy). Each recipe has the name of the author at the bottom of the page. If you like the recipes, please check out Frederico's Facebook Page: https://www.facebook.com/pages/Fredericos/113932728664171 If you want to grow your own food, make your own energy, or do anything green, check out my website at www.sourceofgreenenergy.com.

A few notes about this book. We use organic ingredients as much as possible. You don't have to, of course. If you're going sugar free and gluten free, you may as well go chemical free and go organic. I'm not big into measuring. I prefer to cook by taste, therefore; all of the measurements are approximate. Feel free to substitute and adjust to your taste. Baking is a little different and does require close measurements. You will want to follow those directions as close as possible. This book is for you, so make the recipes yours, after all; everyone's taste buds are different.

We are already working on a second gluten and sugar free cookbook. It will have more Chefs participating and more baking. If you enjoy this one, watch for the next one!

Biographies

Chris Guebert

Hi, I'm Chris Guebert. I have been an Electrical Engineer for over 20 years. I am now the President and CEO of My Green Earth LLC. We cover everything green on our website www.sourceofgreenenergy.com.   We have plans for a dome green house and aquaponics for you to grow your own fruits and vegetables.

I have always loved to cook. I have not had any training. I learned at home as a teenager. The recipes I put in the book are recipes I make a lot and some that I have come up with as my creativity kicked in. People have always liked them. I hope you do too. I do eat sugar free, gluten free and organic. I have my cheat days though.

Find us at:

www.sourceofgreenenergy.com
www.facebook/mygreenearthllc
twitter: @mygreenearthllc
You Tube Channel: mygreenearthllc
Google+: My Green Earth LLC

Frederico Braho

Freddy worked at Italian Restaurants in Germany and Greece. He also trained in Milan, Italy. He moved to the USA and opened his restaurant in 2005. He's living the American Dream! Freddy's food is excellent. When you go to his restaurant, he usually comes out and talks to you. That's how we met. We talked cooking a few times. I had already enlisted some friends who were chefs but, they backed out. That worked out well because it gave me the opportunity to ask Freddy to be part of this book. He provided a lot of great recipes!! If you're in Waterloo, Illinois, stop into his restaurant. You'll love it!

https://www.facebook.com/pages/Fredericos/113932728664171

Frederico's is located at:

1551 N Illinois Route 3
Waterloo, IL

Recipes

Seafood

Asian Talapia

Ingredients:

24 oz fresh wild caught Talapia fillets
Spike seasoning

Sauce:

2 medium cloves of garlic, minced, organic
1 tsp coconut oil, organic, virgin
1/2 tsp ginger , organic
1/2 tsp dijon mustard, organic
2 tbs Soy Sauce, organic (or Coconut Aminos)
1tsp of coconut manna (also called coconut butter) as thickener (you can also use coconut flour or almond flour)
Juice from 1/2 of a small lemon, organic

Instructions:

Sprinkle a little Spike seasoning (or anything else you'd like to try) on the talapia fillets. You can pan fry, bake or grill. Make sure the fish flakes when you stick a fork in it.

Sauce:

Add oil to small pan and put it on low to medium heat (I use 3 of 7 on my stove). add garlic and ginger. Heat for a couple minutes, mixing up the ingredients. Add mustard and soy sauce. Mix in the pan. When the liquid is boiling, add coconut manna (or whichever thickener you chose) and lemon juice. Mix the ingredients and cook until it thickens a bit. Pour over the cooked fish. Enjoy! Feel free to use other fish too.

 by Chris Guebert www.sourceofgreenenergy.com

Breaded Cod

Ingredients:

Wild Caught Cod
Almond Flour/Meal
Sea Salt (I use Himalayan pink salt)
Pepper, Organic
Garlic Powder, Organic
Turmeric, Organic
Coconut Milk, Organic (you can use butter milk, or almond milk)

Instructions:

Pour a little Coconut Milk on a plate (enough to cover the bottom). Pour the Almond
flour on another plate. Mix in the salt, pepper, garlic powder, and turmeric (you can ad a
little cayenne pepper too). I purposely didn't put amounts here. It's up to you. Taste as
you mix. Dip the cod in the milk, on both sides. Then dip the cod in the flour mix, on
both sides. Now it's ready to cook. You have choices. You can deep fry, pan fry, or air
fry in a convection oven. I used the convection oven for the cod in the picture. It's
crisper when you fry it in oil, but good both ways. Enjoy!

by Chris Guebert www.sourceofgreenenergy.com

Dijon Salmon

Ingredients:

2 Wild Caught Salmon Fillets
1 Tbs Organic Dijon Mustard
1 Clove Organic Garlic, minced
2 Tbs Coconut Nectar

Instructions:

Cook the Salmon fillets however you want (grill, skillet, bake). I cooked mine in my convection oven. Add mustard, garlic and coconut nectar to a small sauce pan. Heat on low heat until its warm, stirring the entire time. Pour over the salmon when it's hot. To make it spicier, add more mustard and less coconut nectar. Enjoy!

by Chris Guebert   www.sourceofgreenenergy.com

Grouper

Ingredients:

10-12 Oz of Wild Caught Grouper Fillets
2 C Organic Chicken Stock
1/2 C Organic, Dry White Wine
1/2 Stick of Butter
1 Tbs Organic, Fresh Squeezed Lemon Juice
1 Can Organic Artichoke Hearts
Sprinkle of Parsley
A few Oz of organic rice flour or coconut flour

Instructions:

Coat the grouper in flour. Fry in olive oil (or coconut oil for a healthier version). Boil the wine, stock, and tomato. Reduce it to about half. Add the butter, artichoke and lemon juice. Boil for a couple minutes. Pour over the grouper. Enjoy!

By Freddy from Frederico's Italian Restaurant in Waterloo, IL.
https://www.facebook.com/pages/Fredericos/113932728664171

Grilled Salmon with Roasted Cauliflower

Ingredients:

1 Head of Organic Cauliflower, cleaned and diced
2 Tbs Virgin Organic Olive Oil
1/2 Tsp Sea Salt
1/4 C Organic Minced Shallots (finely Minced)
1 Tsp Organic Minced Garlic
1/2 C Organic Grated Parmesan
4 6-8 oz Wild Caught Salmon Fillets
2 Red Peppers

Instructions:

Roast the cauliflower, olive oil, salt shallots and garlic at 325 Degrees for 25-30 minutes. Add the parmesan and crush together. Coat the red peppers with olive oil and roast for 15-20 minutes at 350 Degrees. After roasting, clean the seeds and skin. Blend the peppers into a sauce. Grill the salmon with olive oil and salt and pepper. Spoon the crushed mixture onto plates. Put the salmon on top. Pour the pepper sauce over the salmon. Enjoy!

Here's a similar recipe:

Salmon with Broccoli Mash

Ingredients:

1 lb Fresh, Organic Broccoli Flowerets
1/4 C Organic Minced Shallots
2 Tbs Extra Virgin Olive Oil
2 C Organic, Low Sodium, Chicken Stock
1 Tsp Organic Minced Garlic
1/2 C Organic Grated Parmesan
1/4 C White Wine (Organic if you can find it)
4 6-8 oz Wild Caught Salmon Fillets

Instructions:

Sauté the oil, shallots, garlic, and, broccoli. Add the white wine and chicken stock. Simmer for 20 minutes, covered. After the liquid evaporates, crush the broccoli, shallots, etc and add the parmesan. Scoop on a plate. Grill the salmon (while the rest is cooking). Place the salmon on top. Enjoy!

By Freddy from Frederico's Italian Restaurant in Waterloo, IL.
https://www.facebook.com/pages/Fredericos/113932728664171

Savory Bacon Wrapped Salmon

Ingredients:

2 Wild Caught Salmon Fillets
1 Tbs Organic Dijon Mustard
1 Clove Organic Garlic, minced
2 Tbs Coconut Aminos
1/2 - 1 Tbs Butter (real, grassfed butter)
2 Slices of Organic Bacon

Instructions:
Wrap the salmon with the 2 slices of bacon. Cook the salmon fillets however you want (grill, skillet, bake). I cooked mine in my convection oven. Add mustard, garlic , butter, and coconut aminos to a small sauce pan. Heat on low heat until its warm, stirring the entire time. Pour over the salmon when it's hot. To make it spicier, add more mustard and less coconut nectar. Enjoy!

 by Chris Guebert   www.sourceofgreenenergy.com

Aranchini

Ingredients:

1/2 Organic Arborio Rice
2 C Water (lightly salted)
1/2 Seafood (mix of chopped shrimp, crab, or whatever you want)
1 Organic, Free Range Egg
1/4 C Gluten Free bread crumbs (or Almond Flour)
1/4 Tsp Organic Garlic Powder
1/2 Tsp Organic, Minced Basil
1/4 C Organic, Grated Parmesan
3 Tbs Organic Tomato Sauce (or Crushed tomatoes)

Instructions:

Boil the rice for 7-8 minutes. Rinse. Add the seafood (whatever you chose, chopped).
Mix all the ingredients together, except the bread crumbs/almond flour. Shape into
balls. Roll the balls in the bread crumbs/almond flour. Deep Fry at 350 Degrees until
golden brown (3-4 minutes). Enjoy!

By Freddy from Frederico's Italian Restaurant in Waterloo, IL.
https://www.facebook.com/pages/Fredericos/113932728664171

Meat

Orange Duck

Ingredients:

2 duck breast, organic

Marinade:
2 cloves mince garlic, organic
juice from 1 orange, organic
1/2 C Coconut Aminos (or Soy Sauce), organic

Instructions:

Add garlic, coconut aminos, and orange juice to pan or plastic bag (whatever you want to use to marinade). Mix the ingredients. Score (slight cuts) the skin of the duck breast. Add the duck breast to the marinade. Marinade over night, flipping the breast half way through. My preference is to grill the duck breast. If you do, remember that duck breast has a lot of fat and will cause a lot of flame ups. You can also cook in a pan or in the oven too (works well in a convection oven). Enjoy!

You can also inject this marinade into a whole duck and smoke it. Taste phenomenal!!

  by Chris Guebert www.sourceofgreenenergy.com

Grilled Steak with a Rub

(Strip steak before grilling)

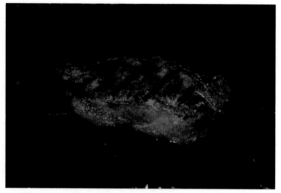

(Strip steak after grilling)

Ingredients:

Ribeye Steak (New York strip or whatever you prefer will work just fine too), grass fed, organic (as many as you'd like)
Sea Salt (I use Himalayan pink salt)
Pepper, organic
Garlic Powder, organic
Spike Seasoning

Instructions:

Sprinkle a little pepper over one side of the steak. Add a nice coating (not too much) of garlic powder over your steak. Add a thick coating of Spike seasoning over your steak. Flip your steak and do the same to the other side. Now let the steak sit in the refrigerator for at least 8 hours (24 is better). Get your steak out and let it sit, at room temperature, for 1 hour before cooking. Heat up the grill before adding your steak. After the steak has cooked for a few minutes, add a little sea salt, if you'd like. When you've finished cooking your steak, take it off the grill and let it sit for 10 minutes before cutting it. Enjoy!

 by Chris Guebert   www.sourceofgreenenergy.com

Marinated Grilled Steak

Ingredients:

Ribeye Steak (New York strip or whatever you prefer will work just fine too), grass fed, organic (as many as you'd like)
Aminos (or Organic Soy Sauce, if you'd prefer)
Minced Garlic, organic
Thyme, organic

Instructions:

Mix the Aminos, minced garlic, and thyme into a marinade. I used 1/2 cup aminos, 2 cloves garlic, and 1/2 tsp of thyme for 2 steaks. Add the steaks to the marinade. Now let the steak sit in the refrigerator for at least 8 hours (24 is better). Get your steak out and let it sit, at room temperature, for 1 hour before cooking. Heat up the grill before adding your steak. After the steak has cooked for a few minutes. When you've finished cooking your steak, take it off the grill and let it sit for 10 minutes before cutting it. Enjoy!

 by Chris Guebert   www.sourceofgreenenergy.com

Award Winning Chili

Ingredients:

2 lbs Organic Grass Fed Ground Beef (Turkey will work too)
4 cloves Organic Garlic
1/2 Organic Small Yellow Onion (or whatever type you want)
1 Tbs Organic Coconut Oil
2 Heaping Tbs Organic Cumin
3 Heaping Tbs Organic Chili Powder
2 Chopped Organic Jalapeños (or more if you want it hot)
2 14 oz cans of Organic Tomato Sauce
2 Organic Yellow Squash (optional)
1/2 can Organic Pumpkin Puree

Instructions:

Add coconut oil, garlic (minced) and chopped onion to your pot. When the oil is warm, add ground beef and brown. Add spices. Stir it all together. Add tomato sauce and jalapeños. Add pumpkin puree (makes it creamier). Chop squash into small pieces and add. Stir everything together. I use a pressure cooker. Seal and cook on low for 15 minutes after the pressure is up. If you would rather cook in a pot, cook 1-2 hours on low heat, stirring often. You can always leave out the squash or use beans instead. To make a chilimac, make spaghetti squash and pour the chili over it. Enjoy!

by Chris Guebert   www.sourceofgreenenergy.com

Tri Tip Roast

Ingredients:

1.5-3 lbs Grassfed Organic Trip Tip Roast
3-4 cloves of organic Garlic, minced
1/2 C Coconut Aminos (or Soy Sauce)
4-5 Organic Carrots
1 small Butternut Squash
3 Tbs Organic Coconut Flour
1 Tbs Coconut Oil

Instructions:

Place the Coconut oil in a pan and turn the heat all the way up. Sear the roast for 1 1/2 to 2 minutes on each side. Place the minced garlic and the aminos in a crock pot. Place the seared roast in the crockpot. Cut the carrots up as you'd like (I cut them in 2 inch pieces). Peel and cut up the butternut squash in an size you'd like (I cut into 1-2 inch pieces). Place both the carrots and squash into the crock pot. Cook on low for 8-12 hours. Turn off the heat. Take the meat, carrots, and squash out (it will all be so tender it's falling apart). Pour the rest into a pan and put on medium heat. Add the coconut flour and stir. It will thicken in a minute or two. Stir the whole time. Now you have gravy. Enjoy!

 by Chris Guebert   www.sourceofgreenenergy.com

BBQ Chicken Wings

Ingredients:

Chicken wings and or drummies
Spike Seasoning
BBQ Sauce (from earlier in this book)

Instructions:

Sprinkle Spike Seasoning on your chicken wings. I like to put a good coating on, but you don't have to. Cook your wings. You can cook them on the grill, in a convection oven, a regular oven, or fry them. If you chose to fry them, coconut oil is the healthiest option. You can apply the sauce by brush (this can brush off the seasoning). I like to pour it on. These wings will be as good as any you get in a restaurant. Enjoy!

If you have a smoker, smoke these and they will be even better!

 by Chris Guebert   www.sourceofgreenenergy.com

Orange Glazed Chicken

Ingredients:

Chicken Thighs (you can use breast, legs, or anything)
Juice from 1 Organic Orange
Coconut Nectar
1-2 cloves Organic Minced Garlic
2-4 Tbs of Coconut Aminos

Instructions:

Bake or grill your chicken. Make the glaze by adding orange juice, coconut nectar, garlic and aminos to a sauce pan. Cook on low heat (175 Degrees) until it starts to thicken. Cover chicken and cook for 2 minutes. If there's sauce left, pour over the chicken as you serve. Enjoy!

 by Chris Guebert   www.sourceofgreenenergy.com

Mexican Burger

Ingredients:

1 Lbs Organic, Grass Fed Ground Beef
1-2 Tbs Organic Coconut Oil
1 Tbs Ground Cumin
4 Oz Organic Taco Sauce
4 oz Organic Cheddar Cheese
3 Tbs Slice Organic Jalapeños (or more if you want it hot)
1 16 Oz Jar of Organic Salsa

Instructions:

Brown the hamburger in the coconut oil adding cumin as it cooks. When the hamburger is browned, add taco sauce and warm for a minute. Spoon onto plate or serving tray. Sprinkle the cheddar cheese over the top. Allow it a couple minutes to melt. Spoon on all the jalapeños you want. Spoon the salsa over the top. You can eat this as a dip or as a meal. Enjoy!

Options: Add a layer of organic sour cream.
              Add a layer of guacamole

by Chris Guebert   www.sourceofgreenenergy.com

Creamy Italian Chicken

Ingredients:

3/4 lbs Organic, Free Range, Chicken Thighs
1 Tbs Organic Coconut Oil
2 Oz Organic Pancetta (you can use Bacon as a substitute)
2 Tsp Organic Minced Garlic
1 Tsp Organic Italian Seasoning
1/2 C Organic Sliced Baby Portobello Mushrooms
1/2 C Organic Cream (or milk of your choice - coconut, almond, cow, goat)
Dash of Organic Paprika
Dash of Organic Pepper
1 Tsp Coconut Aminos (or Soy Sauce)

Instructions:

Add coconut oil, garlic and pancetta to a pan on medium high heat. Cook for a minute or two before adding the cut up chicken thighs. As you cook, add the Italian seasoning. When the chicken is almost finished, add the mushrooms, pepper, and paprika. When everything is cooked, add the cream and coconut aminos and continue to cook for 5 minutes. You can eat it like this, or pour over pasta or spaghetti squash. Enjoy!

by Chris Guebert   www.sourceofgreenenergy.com

Italian Chicken/Bacon Stew

Ingredients:

1 lb Organic, Free Range, Ground Chicken
1-2 Tbs Organic Coconut Oil
3 Slices Organic Bacon (you can use Pancetta as a substitute)
1 Tsp Organic Garlic Powder (minced garlic will work too)
1/2-1 C Organic Sliced Baby Portobello Mushrooms (any organic mushroom will work)
Organic Sea Salt and Organic Pepper to taste
12-1 C Organic Spaghetti Sauce

Instructions:

Add coconut oil, bacon, and mushrooms to a pan on medium high heat. Add salt, pepper and garlic. Cook for 3-4 minutes before adding the ground chicken. When everything is cooked, add spaghetti sauce and continue to cook for 5 minutes. You can make this thin like a meat sauce or thick as a meal itself.   You can eat it like this, or pour over pasta or spaghetti squash. Enjoy!

 by Chris Guebert   www.sourceofgreenenergy.com

Chicken Cacciatore

Ingredients:

4 Organic, Free Range, Chicken Quarters (legs and thighs)
1/2 Organic Chopped Yellow Onion
1 C Organic Fresh Cut Julian Style Red Peppers
1/2 C Organic Fresh Cut Julian Style Yellow Peppers
10 Oz Organic Diced Tomatoes with Juice
1 Tsp Organic Dried Oregano
1 C Ground Tomatoes
1 C Organic Chicken Stock (Low Sodium)
1/2 C White Wine
1 C Organic Rice Flour
1/2 C Organic Extra Virgin Olive Oil
1/2 Tbs Organic Garlic Powder
Organic Sea Salt/Organic Pepper

Instructions:

Roll the chicken in the flour. Pan sear the chicken. Set aside. Sauté vegetables until the onions are translucent. Put in an oven safe dish. Add the wine, followed by the rest of the ingredients. Add the chicken. Spoon some sauce over the chicken and bake for 45 minutes at 350 degrees (flip the chicken over at 30 minutes). Enjoy!

By Freddy from Frederico's Italian Restaurant in Waterloo, IL.
https://www.facebook.com/pages/Fredericos/113932728664171

Turkey Bacon Scramble

Ingredients:

1 lb Organic, Free Range Ground Turkey
3 Slices of Organic Bacon (turkey, pork or beef. Add 1 Tbs Coconut oil if you don't use pork bacon)
6-9 Free Range, Organic Eggs
1/2-1 C Organic Sliced Portobello Mushrooms (or what ever type you like)
1Tsp Organic Cumin
Salt and Pepper to taste

Instructions:

Add the bacon to a pan for 2-3 minutes over medium high heat. Add the mushrooms for 3-4 more minutes. Add salt, pepper, and cumin. Add eggs to a bowl and scramble until well mixed. I used 6 eggs in the picture. 9 might be better if you like eggs. Add eggs to the pan and stir in. Cook until the eggs are cooked. Enjoy!

You can serve this many ways. You can serve it with a sauce - Hollandaise, BBQ (I know...but t taste great!), gravy or any other you can think of.

 by Chris Guebert   www.sourceofgreenenergy.com

Glazed Duck

Ingredients:

2 duck breast, organic

Marinade/Glaze:
2 cloves mince garlic, organic
1/2+ C Organic Coconut Nectar (add more to make it thicker)
1/2 C Coconut Aminos (or Soy Sauce), organic

Instructions:

Add garlic, coconut aminos, and coconut nectar to pan or plastic bag (whatever you want to use to marinade). Mix the ingredients. Score (slight cuts) the skin of the duck breast. Add the duck breast to the marinade. Marinade over night, flipping the breast half way through. My preference is to grill/smoke the duck breast. If you do, remember that duck breast has a lot of fat and will cause a lot of flame ups. You can also cook in a pan or in the oven too (works well in a convection oven).   You can also use some of this marinade/glaze to pour over the duck breast when serving or brush on just before it's finished cooking. Enjoy!

You can also inject this marinade into a whole duck and smoke it. Taste phenomenal!!

 by Chris Guebert   www.sourceofgreenenergy.com

Pasta

Seafood Pasta

Ingredients:

2 oz Organic Extra Virgin Olive Oil (you can use Coconut Oil)
1Tsp Organic fresh minced Garlic
1 Tsp Sea Salt (I use Himalayan pink salt)
1 Tsp Organic Pepper
2-3 oz Dry White Wine
6 oz Clam Juice or Clam stock
pinch of organic crushed Chili Pepper
10 Medium Shrimp
8-10 oz Wild White Fish
1/2 C Organic sliced Mushrooms
1/2 C Organic diced Roma Tomatoes or peeled Tomatoes
Pinch of organic, fresh chopped Parsley
1 Tbs Organic Butter
5-6 oz Linguini (Heartland Gluten free is good) (You can also use spaghetti squash)

Instructions:

Add oil, garlic, salt, pepper, chili pepper, shrimp, fish, mushrooms, tomatoes, parsley
and butter to a pan and sauté. Add wine and clam stock. Boil the linguini in water with
a bit if sea salt and a bit of oil. Add linguini to the pan. Mix all together. Enjoy!

By Freddy from Frederico's Italian Restaurant in Waterloo, IL.
https://www.facebook.com/pages/Fredericos/113932728664171

Turkey Spaghetti Squash

Ingredients:

1 1/2-2 Lbs Organic, Free Range ground Turkey
2-3 cloves of Organic minced Garlic
1-2 Tbs Organic Coconut Oil
1 Tsp Organic dried onion (or half a small fresh onion)
1 Tsp Organic Oregano
1 Tsp Organic Italian Seasoning
Pinch of Sea Salt (I use Himalayan pink salt)
Pinch of Organic Pepper
1 14oz can of Organic Tomato Sauce
1/2 C of Organic sliced Mushrooms
1/4 C Organic Parmesan Cheese
1 Spaghetti Squash

Instructions:

Preheat oven to 425. Split the spaghetti squash in half. Clean out all the seeds. You want to make sure there's nothing but firm flesh left. Pour a little coconut oil over the inside. Spread it around. Add a little salt and pepper. Put in a the oven, face up on a cookie sheet, for roughly 45 minutes. Scrape the inside with a fork. You will see it start to look like spaghetti.

Add coconut oil, garlic, and onion to a pan and warm. Add Turkey, oregano, and italian seasoning. Brown. Add salt, pepper, mushrooms and tomato sauce. Here is where you get to chose. It will be very thin liquid at this point. You can bring it to a boil for 5 minutes if you like it thin or cook for 20 minutes if you like it thick. It's thick in the picture. Spoon over spaghetti squash. Sprinkle parmesan over the top. Enjoy!

 by Chris Guebert   www.sourceofgreenenergy.com

Seafood Lasagna

Ingredients:

1/2 lb Shrimp, diced
1 lb Whitefish (Wild Caught) or Salmon (also Wild Caught)
1/2 lb Crab Meat
1 Organic Medium Onion, chopped
2 Organic Celery Stalks
1 C Organic Chopped Italian Parsley
2 C Organic Parmesan
2 C Organic Ricotto
2 C Gluten Free Flour (coconut will work well) and milk (bash-meal)
4 C Organic Tomato Sauce or Ground Tomatoes
2 lbs Gluten Free Lasagna Noodles
10-15 Fresh Organic Basil Leaves, chopped
2 C Organic, Finely Chopped Mushrooms (Optional)
1 Tsp Organic Minced Garlic
1 Tsp Organic Sea Salt/Organic Pepper
2 Tbs Organic Olive Oil (or Organic Coconut Oil)

Instructions:

Sauté oil with onion in a pan. Add seafood and garlic. Cook partially (don't overcook, since this will bake too). Take the pan off the heat. In an 8X12 pan, add a light layer of tomato sauce, then pasta, followed by bash-meal, seafood and cheese. Make 2-4 layers (4 is better). Bake for 35 Minutes at 375 Deg. Enjoy!

By Freddy from Frederico's Italian Restaurant in Waterloo, IL.
https://www.facebook.com/pages/Fredericos/113932728664171

Meat Lasagna

Ingredients:

1 1/2 lb Organic Sausage
1 1/2 lb Organic Grass Fed Ground Beef
1 Organic Medium Onion, chopped
2 Organic Celery Stalks
1 C Organic Chopped Italian Parsley
2 C Organic Parmesan
2 C Organic Ricotto
2 C Gluten Free Flour (coconut will work well) and milk (bash-meal)
4 C Organic Tomato Sauce or Ground Tomatoes
2 lbs Gluten Free Lasagna Noodles
10-15 Fresh Organic Basil Leaves, chopped
2 C Organic, Finely Chopped Mushrooms (Optional)
1 Tsp Organic Minced Garlic
1 Tsp Organic Sea Salt/Organic Pepper
2 Tbs Organic Olive Oil (or Organic Coconut Oil)

Instructions:

Sauté oil with onion in a pan. Add sausage, ground beef, and garlic. Cook partially (don't overcook, since this will bake too). Take the pan off the heat. In an 8X12 pan, add a light layer of   tomato sauce, then pasta, followed by bash-meal, seafood and cheese. Make 2-4 layers (4 is better). Bake for 35 Minutes at 375 Deg. Enjoy!

By Freddy from Frederico's Italian Restaurant in Waterloo, IL.
https://www.facebook.com/pages/Fredericos/113932728664171

Chicken Alfredo

Ingredients:

4-5 Oz of Gluten Free Penne Pasta (Heartland is a good brand)
1 C Organic Heavy Cream
1/2 Tsp Sea Salt
Pinch of Organic Ground Black Pepper
Pinch of Organic Chopped Parsley (optional, for color)
1/4 C Organic Grated Parmesan
1 Clove of Organic Garlic, Minced
1/2 C Organic, Free Range Chicken (or Shrimp)
1/2 C Organic Vegetables (your choice), cooked (optional)

Instructions:

Cook your chicken (or shrimp) by sautéing, grilling, or steaming. Set it aside. Boil the pasta in water, with a pinch of sea salt, on a low boil, for 10 minutes. Set it aside. Simmer the cream, salt, pepper, parsley, parmesan, and garlic for 2-3 minutes. Add the chicken, vegetable (if desires), and pasta and simmer for 2-3 more minutes. Enjoy!

By Freddy from Frederico's Italian Restaurant in Waterloo, IL.
https://www.facebook.com/pages/Fredericos/113932728664171

Lamb Shanks and Pasta

Ingredients:

7 Oz of Gluten Free Linguini (Heartland is a good brand)
4 12-16 oz Organic Lamb Shanks
1 C Diced Organic Onions
1 C Organic Celery, chopped
1 C Organic Chopped Carrots
3 C Diced Organic Tomatoes with Juice
2 C Organic Ground Tomatoes
2 Tbs Organic Chicken Base
2 C Organic Chicken Stock
2 C Organic Beef Stock
1 Cinnamon Stick
3-4 Cloves Organic Garlic, Minced
2 Bay Leaves
2 Fresh, Organic Basil Leaves
1 C Olive Oil (or coconut oil for a little different taste)

Instructions:

Sauté the lamb shanks on medium/high heat in oil until brown. Set it aside. Sauté the onions, celery, carrots and garlic until the onions are translucent. Add the rest of the ingredients, except the lamb and pasta. Bring to a boil and add the lamb. Cook at 325 degrees for 3 1/2 to 3:45 hours. Boil the pasta in water, with a pinch of sea salt, on a low boil, for 10 minutes. Serve over the pasta. Enjoy!

By Freddy from Frederico's Italian Restaurant in Waterloo, IL.
https://www.facebook.com/pages/Fredericos/113932728664171

Smoothies

Blueberry, Cranberry Smoothie

Ingredients:

1/2 C Organic Blueberries
1/2 C Organic Cranberries
1 Tbs Organic Dark Cherry Juice (any cherry juice will do)
1 Organic Banana
1 C Spinach
1/2 C Coconut Kefir
1/2 C Coconut Milk (Any raw milk will do)
1 Tsp Cinnamon
1 handful or raw, organic walnuts

Instructions:

Add all ingredients and blend. This is an extremely health and very tasty drink. Try different ingredients.   Enjoy!

Remember, cinnamon counters the effects of the sugar from the fruit.

  by Chris Guebert   www.sourceofgreenenergy.com

Strawberry Smoothie

Ingredients:

4-5 Organic Strawberries
1 small container of Greek Yogurt (about 5 oz)
1 Tbs Organic Honey (or Coconut Nectar)
1 Organic Banana (frozen if you want it extra thick)
2 Tbs Organic Cashew Butter
1 C Coconut Milk (Any raw milk will do)
1 Tsp Cinnamon, optional
1 scoop of protein powder

Instructions:

Add all ingredients and blend. This is a smoothie for 1. Double, triple or quadruple the size. Try different ingredients.   Enjoy!

 by Chris Guebert   www.sourceofgreenenergy.com

Pumpkin Smoothie

Ingredients:

1 Tsp Organic Pumpkin Pie Spice
1 Tsp Organic Nutmeg
1/2 can Organic Pumpkin
1 Organic, Frozen Banana
2 Tbs Organic Cashew Butter
1 C Coconut Milk (Any raw milk will do)
1 Tsp Cinnamon, optional

Instructions:

Add all ingredients and blend. This is a smoothie for 1. Double, triple or quadruple the size. Try different ingredients.   Enjoy!

 by Chris Guebert   www.sourceofgreenenergy.com

Category Free!

BBQ/Steak Sauce

Ingredients:

24 oz organic ketchup (best if unsweetened)
10 oz organic worcestershire sauce
1/2 cup of organic apple cider vinegar
4 medium to large cloves of garlic, minced, organic
1/2 tbs fresh onion (I use a few dashes of dried minced onion), organic
2 tbs honey, organic, unfiltered preferred
1 tbs liquid smoke
1/2 tsp Trader Joe's African Smoke seasoning
a dash or 2 of cayenne pepper or chipolte pepper (it's mild this way, ad more to make it hotter), organic
sea salt and organic pepper to taste (I use roughly 1/2 tsp each)

Instructions:

Add all ingredients into a pan (I usually add the liquids, turn on the heat and add the other ingredients). Bring to a low boil (I set my stove on 3 out of 7). Then low heat to simmer. Simmer for 1 hour, stirring often. Last, this step is optional, blend until it's a smooth liquid. This makes a tangy sauce, not too sweet or smoky. Adjust to your own taste buds. Enjoy!

This is a tangy BBQ sauce. To make it less tangy, add less apple cider vinegar. To make it sweeter, add more honey, and less apple cider vinegar. To make it hotter, add more pepper.

 by Chris Guebert   www.sourceofgreenenergy.com

Lo Mein?

Ingredients:

1 Spaghetti Squash, Organic
Coconut Oil, organic
Sea Salt (I use Himalayan pink salt)
Pepper, Organic
1Tbs butter, organic grass fed
1Tsp Minced Garlic, organic
1/4 tsp Turmeric, organic (Optional)
Soy Sauce, organic or Aminos

Instructions:

Preheat oven to 425. Split the spaghetti squash in half. Clean out all the seeds. You want to make sure there's nothing but firm flesh left. Pour a little coconut oil over the inside. Spread it around. Add a little salt and pepper. Put in a the oven, face up on a cookie sheet, for roughly 45 minutes. It is done when you stick it with a fork and its very soft. If you use a convection oven like I do, it will be faster and you may not need a cookie sheet. Take it out and let it cool a little (it's too hot to handle). Scrape the inside with a fork. You will see it start to look like spaghetti.

Add butter to a wok or pan. Melt butter at a high heat (I set mine on 5 out of 7). Add Garlic and turmeric. Add the soy sauce as everything else start cooking pretty fast. Turn the heat down to simmer. Take a fork and rake it across the inside of the squash. It actually looks like spaghetti (or Lo Mein noodles). Get all of it out that you can and add it to the wok. Stir it in with the sauce. Turn off the heat. Now you have Lo Mein without any gluten.   You can add ingredients (to make it any kind of Lo Mein you want, beef, chicken, veggies, etc.) before adding the squash. Enjoy!

  by Chris Guebert   www.sourceofgreenenergy.com

Pizza Dough

Ingredients:

1 C Water
1 pack of yeast
1/2 tsp Sea Salt (I use Himalayan pink salt)
2 C Gluten free Flour (Bob's Red Mill Biscuit and Baking Mix)
1 Tbs Virgin, organic coconut oil (melted)

Instructions:

Mix the yeast in the warm water (a little over 100 Deg) until it dissolves. Put 2 cups of flour into a bowl. Add salt. Add water and yeast and mix, by hand at least 30 strokes. Pour the oil (you don't have to measure it precisely) over the dough, and turn, making sure the oil covers the dough. Let it stand, covered for 20 minutes. Spread the dough into a pizza pan, stone, or cookie sheet. Add whatever pizza sauce, toppings and cheese you like. Cook 10-20 minutes (depending on how thick you decide to make it) at 400 degrees. One tip: to add flavor, add garlic and oregano to the crust or sauté mushrooms in coconut oil or grass fed, organic butter and add minced garlic and oregano to them while cooking. It's a great pizza topping. Enjoy!

  by Chris Guebert   www.sourceofgreenenergy.com

Fried Rice? No, Quinoa

Ingredients:

1 C Organic Quinoa
2 C Broth, organic, chicken or beef
1 clove of organic Garlic, minced
2 Tbs Coconut Aminos (or Soy Sauce)
1 Organic Carrot, shredded
1/2 C Cabbage, shredded
1/2 C Peas
1/2 C Mushrooms (whatever type you'd like)

Instructions:

Add quinoa, broth, and peas to a pot and bring to a boil. Turn heat to simmer. Simmer, covered for 15 minutes (or until the broth is absorbed). Place the Coconut oil in a pan and turn the heat about 1/3 of the way up. Add the rest of the ingredients and stirfry for a couple minutes (until tender). Now add the cooked quinoa (with the peas) and mix, with the heat on for a couple minutes. Serve. Add Aminos or soy sauce as desired. Enjoy!

by Chris Guebert   www.sourceofgreenenergy.com

Buttered Pecans

Ingredients:

1-2 Handfuls of Raw, Organic Pecans
1-2 Tsp Organic Butter
Sea Salt (I use Himalayan pink salt)

Instructions:

Melt the butter on low heat. Poor over the Pecans. Add a little salt (to your taste). Mix or stir. This is a great,healthy snack. You can try Walnuts too. Enjoy!

  by Chris Guebert   www.sourceofgreenenergy.com

Blueberry Pancakes

Ingredients:

1/2 C Organic Almond Flour/Meal
1/2 C Organic Coconut Flour
1 C Coconut Milk (Almond milk will work just as well)
1 Tsp Organic Vanilla Extract
2 Tbs Organic Baking Powder
1/2 C Organic Blueberries
1 Tbs Lakanto
1 Organic, Free Range Egg
Syrup: Coconut Nectar

Instructions:

Mix 1 egg until it's well blended. Add all the other ingredients (except the blueberries) and blend. When everything else is added, fold in the blueberries. Cook in a pan or on a griddle, just like any other pancakes. Put butter on (if desired) and add coconut nectar. Enjoy!

by Chris Guebert   www.sourceofgreenenergy.com

Veggies

Grilled Squash

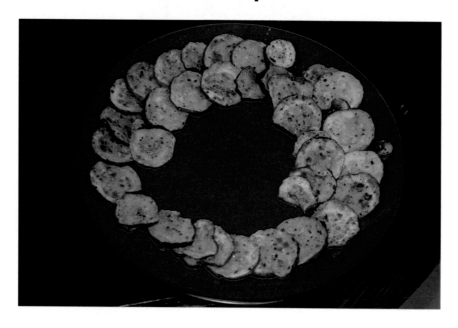

Ingredients:

3 squash, organic (you can use yellow squash and/or zucchini)
Sea Salt
Pepper, organic
Trader Joe's Everyday Seasoning
Coconut Oil, organic, virgin

Instructions:

Cut squash in lengthwise or cross wise direction. Coconut oil is a solid below 76 degrees. If yours in solid, set the jar in warm water for a few minutes. Poor a little oil in a pan or on a plate. Coat both sides of the squash slices in the oil. Don't worry if it turns back into a solid on the squash. It will melt when cooking. Put on a hot grill. You can cook in a pan indoors or out instead, if you'd like or even in a convection oven. Sprinkle salt, pepper and the Everyday Seasoning on top of the squash while the other side is grilling. Flip and add the seasoning to the other side. I grill until the squash is crispy, but you can stop cooking when the squash is soft and somewhat translucent, if you'd prefer. Enjoy!

by Chris Guebert   www.sourceofgreenenergy.com

Vegetable Stir Fry

Ingredients:

Mushrooms, organic (whatever type you like)
Broccoli, organic
Zucchini, organic
Sea Salt (I use Himalayan pink salt)
Garlic Powder, organic
Turmeric, organic
Coconut oil, organic, virgin

Instructions:

Cut zucchini into half circles. Add coconut oil to you pan or wok (there are advantages to using a wok). Use higher heat (I set mine on 5 out of 7). When the pan is warm, add zucchini, then a little salt, garlic powder, and turmeric. Cook for a few minutes, making sure you're cooking both sides. When the zucchini is nearly finished, add the broccoli to the middle of the pan, moving the zucchini out to the outside (this is where a wok is really good). Add a little salt, garlic powder, and turmeric. After a couple of minutes of cooking and stirring, add the mushrooms (slice them first if needed) to the center of the pan, moving the broccoli to the outside with the zucchini. Add a little salt, garlic powder, and turmeric. The mushrooms will only take a couple minutes. Stir everything together and serve. Enjoy!

Feel free to add chicken, shrimp or scallops to this (scallops would be really good).

By the way, turmeric is really good for you, especially at detoxifying your liver.

by Chris Guebert   www.sourceofgreenenergy.com

Grilled Butternut Squash

Ingredients:

1 Organic Butternut Squash
Organic coconut oil
Organic Garlic Power
Organic butter, grass fed cows

Instructions:

Peel the squash. Cut the thinner part into 1/2 inch thick slices. When you get to the thicker part, cut it in half. Scrape out the seeds with a spoon. Cut into pieces that are big enough not to fall through your grill, but not too rounded (you want to have as much contact with the grill as possible). Melt a table spoon or 2 of coconut oil in a pan. Add garlic powder to the oil, sprinkling it evenly. Put the squash in the oil to coat it on all sides. It's OK if the oil goes back to a solid. Put it on the grill on high heat. Flip it when you're half way through. It is done when it's soft when you stick a fork in it. The coconut oil will cause some flame ups. That's OK. Cut up and put butter on top. Enjoy!

 by Chris Guebert   www.sourceofgreenenergy.com

Spinach Pie

Ingredients:

Crust:
1/2 C Organic Rice Flour (You can use coconut flour)
1/2 Stick Organic Butter
3/4 C Milk
1/2 Tsp Sea Salt

Filling:
1/2 Medium Organic Onion, chopped
1 1/2 - 2 lbs Fresh, Organic Spinach
1/4 C Organic Parmesan Cheese, grated
1/2 Tsp Fresh, Chopped, Organic Dill

Instructions:
Ad flour and butter to a bowl. Break the butter up. Mix in the milk and salt. Set aside. Sauté the onions until they are translucent. Add the spinach and dill. Sauté until the spinach is cooked. Remove from the heat and chop. Roll the dough into crust. Cover the bottom and sides of an 18 inch pan. Fill with the filling. Cover the top with the remaining crust. Cut a few holes. Bake at 325 Degrees for 25-30 minutes. Enjoy!

By Freddy from Frederico's Italian Restaurant in Waterloo, IL.
https://www.facebook.com/pages/Fredericos/113932728664171

Dessert

Chocolate Nut Bars

Ingredients:

1 or 2 dark chocolate bars, organic (or more depending on the size of your pan) (You can use dark chocolate chips too)
Coconut oil, organic, virgin
Raw, organic mixed nuts
Sea Salt (I use Himalayan pink salt)
Coconut Nectar (you can also use honey)

Instructions:

Coat the pan (glass or ceramic is fine) with the coconut oil, just enough to keep the chocolate from sticking. Cover the bottom of the pan with the dark chocolate. Don't worry about some empty spaces. The will be covered when the chocolate melts. You can make it as thick as you'd like. Of course, there is the old fashioned way of using a double boiler to melt chocolate too, then pour the melted chocolate into the coated pan. I stick my pan in my convection oven on high for 4 minutes. While the chocolate is cooking, put a handful of mixed nuts in a blender and blend until you have small to medium sized pieces. When the chocolate is melted, let it cool a little. While the chocolate is still soft, but not too hot, pour the nuts over the chocolate. Sprinkle a little sea salt over the chocolate. Poor a little coconut syrup or honey over the nuts. Let it cool and cut into pieces. Option: Ad a layer of raw organic cashew nut butter on top, after it's fully cooled. It's fantastic! Enjoy!

 by Chris Guebert   www.sourceofgreenenergy.com

Chocolate Banana Strawberry Ice Cream

Ingredients:

1/2 C Coconut Milk
1 Tbs Organic Cocoa powder
1/2 Tbs Lakanto (in place of sugar), You can also use honey
2 Organic Bananas, frozen
3-5 Organic Strawberries
1 scoop of Organic Whey Protein

Instructions:

Peel and freeze the bananas (you can peel when frozen, but it's much harder ;-). Add all ingredients to a blender (coconut milk last). Blend until completely liquified (on highest setting). This makes a soft serve. To make it thicker, put it in the freezer for 30 minute to an hour. Do not freeze solid unless you want a big hard ice cube. Obviously, you can alter the flavors significantly. Enjoy!

by Chris Guebert www.sourceofgreenenergy.com

Chocolate Cheesecake

Ingredients:

7 Tbs Organic, Grass Fed Butter
2 C Almond Meal
3 8oz packages of Organic Cream Cheese
1/4 C Organic Coco Powder
3/4 C Coconut Nectar
3 Organic, Free Range Eggs
1 Orange (or half of a large orange)
6 Tbs Coconut Nectar (sauce and crust)
2 Squares Dark chocolate
Zest from 1 Organic Lemon

Instructions:

Melt 4 Tbs butter and add to almond flour and 3 tbs coconut nectar. Mix well and use to form crust (press into pan) in spring form pan or pie pan. Bake for 5-8 minutes at 350 Deg.

Blend 3 Tbs butter, cream cheese, coco powder, Lakanto (or coconut nectar), eggs, lemon zest, and cashew butter together on medium speed until mixed well. Refrigerate for 1 hour. Pour into spring form or pie pan. Bake at 300 Deg for 35-60 minutes.

Add 2 squares of dark chocolate to a warm pan. Add 3 tbs coconut nectar or Lakanto and the juice from 1 small or medium orange. Stir until melted and mixed. This is your sauce. Cool to at least room temp and pout over each piece of cheesecake. Enjoy!

For a creamier version, add 8 oz of sour cream.

by Chris Guebert www.sourceofgreenenergy.com

Chocolate Covered Strawberries

Ingredients:

1 Pint of fresh Organic Strawberries, washed (or however many you want to make)
3 3 oz. Organic Dark Chocolate Bars, Salted if possible (I used Salazon with Sea Salt)
1 C chopped up Raw Organic Almonds (try cashews or other nuts too)
1/2 C Shredded Organic Coconut
a few drops of Organic Peppermint Extract

Instructions:

Break up the chocolate bars into a few pieces and add to a small pot (or a double boiler). Stir often with a spatula until melted. Add Peppermint extract. Stir in the peppermint. If your chocolate doesn't have sea salt added, add a pinch or two (to taste). You just want a little taste of salt. If your chocolate is bitter, add 1 tsp to 1 tbs of coconut nectar to sweeten. Add a little at a time and taste. Make sure the strawberries are dry and start dipping. Then roll in the chopped nuts and coconut. Let them cool on parchment paper. Refrigerate if you don't eat them right away. Enjoy!

  by Chris Guebert   www.sourceofgreenenergy.com

Peanut Butter Chocolate Bars

Ingredients:

1 C Almond Flour
16 Oz Organic (raw if you can find it) Peanut Butter
3/4-1 C Lakanto (Coconut Nectar can also be used)
4 - 3 oz Dark Chocolate Bars with Sea Salt

Instructions:

Mix the peanut butter, almond flour and Lakanto thoroughly. Melt the chocolate over low heat (about 175 deg). If your chocolate doesn't have any sea salt in it, add a small amount. Enjoy!

Option: If you really want to try something different, add 1/4 C of crispy organic bacon bits

                 8 oz of sour cream will make it creamier and give it a different flavor.

by Chris Guebert   www.sourceofgreenenergy.com

Tropical Freeze

Ingredients:

1 Organic Mango, peeled and the seed removed
4 Organic Kiwis (peeled or scooped out)
2 Frozen Organic Bananas, peeled
1 C Organic Coconut Milk
2 Tbs Lakanto (Honey or Coconut Nectar will work too)
1-2 Tbs Organic Cocoa
1 Scoop of Organic Protein Powder (Optional)

Instructions:

Add mango, kiwi, banana Lakanto, Cocoa and Protein Powder (if you use it). Next, add Coconut Milk. Blend on high speed. Don't let it go too long in a high speed blender or it will tun into a whipped cream. This makes a soft serve. You can put it in the freezer for a little while if you want it more firm. Enjoy!

 by Chris Guebert   www.sourceofgreenenergy.com

Coconut Cream Mango Banana Pie

Ingredients:

8 Oz Organic Mango, sliced (you can use peached for a sweeter taste)
1 Organic Banana
14 Oz Coconut Cream
1/2 C Organic, Shredded Coconut
1 Tsp Organic Vanilla Extract
1 Gluten Free, Sugar Free Pie Crust (they are available)

Instructions:

Blend coconut cream (it often separates in the container on the shelf) with the shredded coconut and vanilla extract. Slice the banana. Fold in the banana and the mango. Prepare the crust according to their instructions. Pour the mix into the pie crust and refrigerate for a few hours. It's not pretty but, oh so good! Enjoy!

 by Chris Guebert   www.sourceofgreenenergy.com

Notes

Coconut flour is available in health food stores and some grocery stores.

Coconut Nectar is available on-line, in specialty grocery stores and some health food stores (they can probably order it for you). Same for Coconut Aminos (I use the same brand).

Lakanto can only be ordered on-line. Several on-line stores carry it. We have a link on our website. Do a search and you'll find it too.

Trader Joe's South African Smoke (obvious where you can get it) contains paprika flakes, sea salt, garlic, and basil. You can easily make your own.

Trader Joe's Every Day Seasoning contains sea salt, mustard seeds, black peppercorns, coriander, onion, garlic, paprika, and chili pepper.

You can find Spike Seasoning at many health food stores and at specialty grocery stores.

Bonus Recipes

1. Mix 3 Tbs Almond butter (Cashew butter works well too), 1/2 Tbs cocoa powder, and 1 Tbs Coconut Nectar. You can put this on bread or just eat it with a spoon. It tastes great!!

2. Add 3 Oolong Tea bags and 2 Peppermint Tulsi tea bags to a pitcher. Add 4 cups boiling water. Steep for 5-10 minutes. Remove the tea bags. Add 1/2 Tsp of Stevia. Fill the rest of the pitcher with coconut water. This tastes great and offers lots of health benefits!

3. Cut the stem from a large Portobello mushroom. Place the mushroom on a grill or in an oven, stem side down for 5-7 minutes. Turn over and fill with Spinach and Artichoke dip. This tastes great! We will have a more detailed version of this (recipe for the dip and a pic) in our next cookbook.

Watch for another Gluten and Sugar free cookbook from us soon!